Pocahontas

Library of Congress Control Number: 2018944881
ISBN 978-1-250-16884-9

Our books may be purchased in bulk for promotional, educational, or business use. Please contact your local bookseller or the Macmillan Corporate and Premium Sales Department at (800) 221-7945 ext. 5442 or by email at MacmillanSpecialMarkets@macmillan.com.

First published in France in 2016 by Quelle Histoire, Paris
First U.S. edition, 2019

Text: Patricia Crété
Translation: Catherine Nolan
Illustrations: Bruno Wennagel, Mathieu Ferret, Nuno Alves Rodrigues, Aurélien Fernandez, Aurélie Verdon

Printed in China by RR Donnelley Asia Printing Solutions Ltd., Dongguan City, Guangdong Province

10 9 8 7 6 5 4 3 2 1

Pocahontas

Roaring Brook Press
New York

Growing Up

Pocahontas was born around 1595. She belonged to the Powhatan tribe of Native Americans. Her father was the chief of the tribe. They lived in the part of the United States that is now called Virginia.

Pocahontas's real name was Matoaka. Pocahontas was her nickname, which meant "playful one." Like other young children in the tribe, she worked hard farming corn, beans, and squash, which her people called "the Three Sisters." But she also liked to have a good time!

——

1595–1606

The English Arrive

In May 1607, when Pocahontas was eleven years old, sails appeared on the horizon. Three English ships—the *Susan Constant*, the *Godspeed*, and the *Discovery*—made landfall near Pocahontas's village.

The English people had come to start a colony and look for gold. They built a fort at the water's edge and called it Jamestown.

1607

A Hard Winter

Winter came. It was bitterly cold, and the English struggled to survive. They sent a man named John Smith to ask Pocahontas's father for help.

The Powhatans did not trust John Smith. They took him prisoner and asked him questions before letting him go. Many years later, John Smith said they sentenced him to death but that Pocahontas threw herself in front of him and saved his life. In fact, he likely made up this story.

————

December 1607

Trying for Peace

Pocahontas visited the settlers of Jamestown often. She played with children from the colony and sometimes talked to John Smith.

Her visits had a serious purpose, too. Pocahontas wanted to learn more about the English, and she helped keep peace between the foreigners and her tribe. The colony also borrowed a lot of food and supplies from the Powhatan tribe, and Pocahontas helped the two groups communicate.

1607–1609

Losing Peace

One night in October 1609, John Smith woke up to a loud *boom*! A supply of gunpowder had exploded.

He was badly hurt. He had to go back to England to see doctors there. He left without telling the Powhatans. They later heard that he had died on the voyage home.

About the same time, peace between the English and the Powhatans fell apart. In 1610, war broke out.

———

1609–1610

Taken Prisoner

During the war, Pocahontas was captured by an English captain named Samuel Argall. He made an offer to her father: He would trade Pocahontas for some English prisoners.

But the chief refused. He was worried that if he agreed, the English might kidnap more children.

Pocahontas was taught to speak English. She was also asked to convert to Christianity, but she refused. Then a settler named John Rolfe asked her to marry him. As part of the arrangement, she agreed to accept her new husband's religion.

—

1613–1614

Getting Married

Pocahontas was baptized and took the name Rebecca. She began to wear dresses and hats like an English lady.

On April 5, 1614, she and John Rolfe were married. Their wedding helped end the fighting between the English and the Powhatans. People on both sides were thankful. They called this time the "Peace of Pocahontas."

1614

Starting a Family

The young couple settled near Henricus, another English colony. Soon, Pocahontas gave birth to a baby boy named Thomas.

Pocahontas was invited to visit England with her family. Now she would get to see for herself what England was like!

———

1614–1616

Visiting England

In London, Pocahontas was presented to King James I and his court. They were surprised that she spoke perfect English and knew the rules of their society. As for Pocahontas, she was shocked by the dirt and stink of the city!

John Smith came to see Pocahontas. She could hardly believe he was alive!

——
1616

Falling Ill

After seven months of traveling, the Rolfe family decided to go back to Virginia. The boat left the harbor, but it did not go far. Onboard, Pocahontas had fallen seriously ill. She was taken off the ship for treatment, but nothing helped.

Pocahontas died on March 21, 1617. She was buried in Gravesend, England.

1617

1590

1595
Pocahontas is born.

1607
Jamestown, the first English colony, is founded.

1609
John Smith is wounded and returns to England.

1611
The English start a second colony: Henricus.

1608
Pocahontas prevents a battle by alerting settlers that Native Americans are going to attack.

1610
The English and the Powhatans go to war.

1613
Pocahontas is captured.

1615
Pocahontas gives birth to a son, Thomas.

1616
Pocahontas meets King James I.

1617
Pocahontas dies.

1620

1611
John Rolfe begins farming tobacco.

1614
Pocahontas marries John Rolfe.

1616
Pocahontas and her family arrive in England.

Virginia Colony

North America

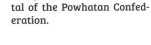

MAP KEY

① Jamestown

Jamestown was the first successful English colony in America, founded in 1607. It was named in honor of King James I.

② Werowocomoco

Pocahontas grew up in this village, which was the capital of the Powhatan Confederation.

③ Henricus

Four years after Jamestown was founded, the English started this second colony. It takes its name from Prince Henry, son of James I.

④ Varina Farms

John Rolfe grew tobacco here and exported it to England.

⑤ Passapatanzy

Pocahontas was captured by Samuel Argall in this village.

⑥ Chickahominy River

John Smith was traveling up this river when he was captured by the Powhatans.

People to Know

Wahunsunacock
(about 1540–1618)

Pocahontas's father was the chief of the Powhatans, a community that included several Native American tribes. He was very powerful.

John Smith
(1580–1631)

The captain fought in many wars before heading to Virginia to help start a colony. When he returned home to England, he wrote books about the Native Americans.

John Rolfe
(1585–1622)
Pocahontas's husband was a very
successful tobacco farmer.

James I
(1566–1625)
James was king of England and Scotland.
During his reign, England began forming
colonies in America.

....

....

Pocahontas was also called Amonute and Matoaka. It was common for Powhatans to have many names. Sometimes they used different names for special occasions or took secret names that only a few people knew.

John Smith exaggerated some of the events in his journals. This is why many historians believe he made up the story about Pocahontas saving his life. Others believe he didn't understand what was happening.

....

Pocahontas had a husband named Kocoum before she married John Rolfe, and she may have had a child.

....

President Woodrow Wilson's wife, Edith Wilson, was a descendant of Pocahontas.

Available Now

 Muhammad Ali

 Marie Antoinette

 Neil Armstrong

 Blackbeard

 Buddha

 Coco Chanel

Charlie Chaplin

 Cleopatra

 Marie Curie

 Albert Einstein

 Anne Frank

 Gandhi

 Frida Kahlo

 Martin Luther King

 Abraham Lincoln

 Nelson Mandela

 Isaac Newton

 Rosa Parks

 Pocahontas

 Vincent van Gogh

Coming Soon

 Joan of Arc

 John F. Kennedy

 Pablo Picasso

 Princess Diana